Advent Calendar
for Couples

24 Days of Beautiful Relationship Moments
>> Small Gestures with Great Effects <<

This Advent calendar
belongs to:

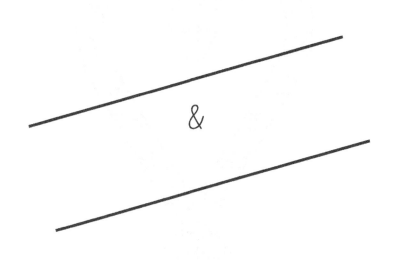

&

Here's how it works:

This Advent calendar is intended to be an impetus for more mutual attention and romance in everyday life.
Each person chooses one of the two characters:

Each Advent day page is assigned to either one character or both and should be turned and read by the respective person in the morning.
Have fun and many beautiful moments!

Post-It
Love messages

Scatter small messages around - e.g. "I love your smile" near the toothbrush.

2

Back massage

Give her/his back some relaxation with a massage - just 10 minutes works wonders.

3

Common paths

Go for a walk together in the fresh air – the more nature surrounds you, the better.

Friends for life

Invite her/his friends to join you – e.g. surprisingly for dinner together.

5

5

Nimble fingers
– tense feet

Give the soles of her/his feet
a little relaxation with a
massage – for example,
during the evening watching
a series together.

Cuddling in the cinema

Go to a recent movie together – even bad movies make for fun memories.

7

Social Media Love Post

Declare your love on social media – alternatively, you can write a romantic text message.

Love goes through the stomach

Prepare a meal with love – e.g. arrange the favorite food in the shape of a heart. Do not forget to decorate the table!

9

9

Bathing fun

Enjoy a bath together
- just be on the same
wavelength again.

10

Pick up surprise

Pick her/him up at quitting time – make sure you know today's schedule.

11

Touching Hug

Give a long and intimate hug – physical contact releases happiness hormones.

12

Indoor picnic

Treat yourself to a picnic in your own living room – a fun experience that will change your perspective.

13

13

Open Sesame!

Share something embarrassing about yourself – open up to deepen your relationship.

14

14

Cry of love

Declare your love in public – e.g. shout from the window, so that even the neighbors no longer have any doubts about your love.

Social games

Play a party game together
- just the two of you or
team up with your loved
ones.

16

Falling asleep fantastically

Tell her/him a bedtime story in which she/he plays the main role – we are all children at heart.

17

Showing teeth

Smile at her/him today in every suitable moment - good vibes only!

18

Fancypants

Spruce yourselves up and go out to eat – ordering pizza in evening dress has its appeal, too.

19

Paper Romance

Write a classic love letter and place it on her/his pillow – add a scent to the letter if you like.

20

Trio of compliments

Give three well-chosen compliments – spread them throughout the day to give pleasure multiple times.

21

Prepared interview

Think of three questions each that you would like to ask each other in the evening - no taboos, wine is allowed.

22

Helping hands

Why don't you take on two household tasks today that you don't usually do (often) – without commenting on it?

23

Somebody's gonna kiss the donkey

Surprise her/him with a passionate kiss – the more unexpected, the better.

24

The we-wellness

Plan (and book!) a date for a joint activity in the new year – e.g. a concert, wellness or pottery classes.

Closing Words:

Hopefully, you've shared some beautiful and memorable moments. By the way, small friendly gestures help to keep your relationship fresh outside the Advent season, too.

If you enjoyed the book, I'd be happy to receive a review.

All the best to you in the new year!

Couple
Advent Calendar
for Parents

24 Days of Beautiful Relationship Moments
>> Couple Time in Everyday Family Life <<

Self-Care
Advent Calendar
for Me

24 Days of Self-Love, Mindfulness,
Gratitude, Relaxation and Serenity,
>> Time to Take Care of Myself <<

Other books you or your friends might also enjoy:

SUDOKU
ADVENT CALENDAR

24 Puzzles
+Solutions

Merry Christmas!
SYMBOL SUDOKU

120 Puzzles
+Solutions

Other books you or your friends might also enjoy:

ISBN: 9798865243335

IMPRINT
THOMAS RÖPER
DAMMANNSTR. 96
45138 ESSEN, GERMANY
ROEPER-THOMAS@WEB.DE

Made in United States
Orlando, FL
27 November 2024